Just Keep Going, Man! Diaries and Reflections of a multiple UK City Tour: Edinburgh, Inverness, The Isle of Sky, Glasgow, Newcastle, London, Belfast, and Portrush.

June to July 27, 2017

By Julian Kasey Jan

My Gratitude

The creative process can be a solitary exercise, but never underestimate the power of good women, and a friend who knows his "stuff." I would like to thank my intellectual entourage of just three: my assistant Shazeda Chowdhury, for her honesty, patience, and integrity while reading my work. To my wife, Melissa, for her input, editing, encouragement, tutelage, and therapeutic love, teaching me how to take a break from my desk and relax once in a while. And last but not least, my editor Bradley Steffens.

Just Keep Going, Man is a log of my experience of encounters, ups, downs, right turns, left turns, wrong turns, and a story about meeting and speaking with a wide variety of strangers of all ages, races, religions, nationalities, and socio-economic classes while I was on a rather long holiday back in my birth country of the United Kingdom. I was also reunited with three old friends that I had not seen in many years. I went to seven major UK cities and discovered a couple more: the Isle of Sky and Portrush. I stayed in nine hotels and traveled 3,000 miles in the United Kingdom, all that by myself. I place some emphasis on the last word because my youth is behind me now. I am married and a middle-aged man with a physical injury. This short book is my diaries and reflections of my trip, and it is a story about my independence, my ability to overcome adversity on the road, reuniting with old friends, and being on an emotional search. I went to many pubs, restaurants, and historic places. Some travel tips are in the book, but by no means is this a travel guide. As the subtitle reflects, it is a story about a trip and never giving up, no matter the circumstances. Besides a few books I read while on and off the road (*Down North: Reflections of Ballymurphy and the Early Troubles* by Ciaran De Baroid; *Belfast Diary: War as a Way of Life* by John Conroy; and *George Michael: The Life 1963-2016* by Emily Herbert), most of the material for this book came from the people I met and the historic places I visited—a great source of material for any writer.

I took this trip because, being an expatriate and living in the State of Qatar, it is a standard common practice for locals and non-residents like myself to take a long summer holiday. My wife, Melissa, and I had talked about going to Croatia, and most of it was planned, but after some soul searching, we could not manage a month-long holiday in Croatia, in part due to her desire to visit our home state of

Michigan. I chose not to go with her to the United States. So putting myself in an emotional and physical state of independence, I did some soul searching of my own. Coming close to a country count of fifty, and with some contentment of world travel, rather than seek out another country to travel too, I decided to go back to Britain.

The trip was my tenth to the UK since I moved to Qatar six years ago. Since my family immigrated to the United States in 1976, I went back to the UK several times as child, and then every year as a teenager. My first solo trip to England was at age twelve, as an un-accompanied minor with my younger brother Nick. After I graduated from college, I moved to London in 1994, and then to Kent in 1997. I then left the UK in 2000. I am in my comfort zone when I am in the UK. It is home.

Therefore, I planned the trip in one sit down. I booked hotels in seven UK cities, in the major ones I have mentioned. I chose the seven cities for various reasons, emotional and practical ones. Edinburgh was a good start and close to Inverness, where I had never been, a city famous for the legendary Loch Ness monster Nessie. Newcastle, I have friends in; Glasgow, I stumbled upon; and London, I am a lifelong Londoner at heart and in experience. As for Belfast, I have a friend who lives there, and I have been curious about the city that was a pivotal one in the Anglo-Irish conflict. I have been an avid reader of British and Irish politics since I was an upperclassman in college. I even earned a graduate degree in British history in 1997 from the University of Westminster in London.

I enjoyed my time in all the places I went to, and I developed some new emotional connections in virtually all the cities I went to in Scotland. While in London, I ran into born-and-bred Londoners (due to extraordinarily high property values Londoners have been pushed out of London, and are fewer in numbers today) and found I was entirely on their mental wavelength, and they on mine. However, the city that gave me an emotional uplift was Belfast. A city in a first world Western country, where conflict was part commonplace and a part of everyday life during the time known as the Troubles (1969 to 1990, roughly), one might expect bitterness. I found the opposite. The British have a saying: "You never know what's around the corner;" neither did I when I got to Belfast, but it is the city that inspired the title of this book, *Just Keep Going, Man!*.

Before *Just Keep Going, Man!* I had been working on my autobiography *American Runaway, the Story of Emigration, Privilege and Loss.* My story about growing up with affluence as the son of a successful physician and investor (my father Dr. Iqbal Jan) in my home state of Michigan and then my living twenty-three years away from it. I have been an expat in several countries: South Korea, Japan, the Dominican Republic, Turkey, and now Qatar. As a non-passport holder of Qatar, I am unable to stay on a permanent basis. I have a residency card as a noncitizen that is up for renewal every year or two. The polite way of putting it is that I am a guest, and the reality is a life in transit, physically and on an emotional basis. Nothing is permanent as an expat, and I develop my thoughts on this in the reflections part and on my feelings about the time, I have spent in Qatar. Some of *Just Keep*

Going, Man! is a precursor of what is to come in autobiography, but that is much longer and even more of a serious story, as I describe my life in one word in the introduction of that book—resilience. As it was never my intention to publish my diaries, this book starts off lighthearted about my trip, later becomes partly autobiographical, then in the middle of it more philosophical and inspirational—a type of self-help book, about overcoming adversity. Something, like many of us, I have had to do, most of my adult life.

In *Just Keep Going, Man!* besides some minor spell check, I left my diaries original. For additional thought, I have added a reflections section. My diaries were written in pubs, restaurants, on trains, and in my hotels in the UK, after street interactions with various people. Whereas with the limited street culture in Doha,[1] most of my reflections

---

[11] Doha is like my home town of Detroit where Car Culture is prevalent. However, for an example of Arabian street life there is a place called Souq (pronounced sook) Waqif. Although the entire area of it can probably fit into a football field, the Souq is pure Arabia in the middle of a busy metropolis. There is a wide open area in the middle, with several entrances north and south to it. As I would describe it, myself, there is a north entrance. It has shops that sell Arabic handcrafts, and has some Western coffee shops like the Coffee Beanery. There is also a stand and a tea shop called Tea Time that sells my favorite Arabic tea, karak, which is tea boiled in milk. When drinking it, the taste is very sweet. So much that when drinking it, it is like consuming some type of dessert. It costs only a few riyals for a cup, whereas a cup at the Western coffee shops is six times the price. As one continues into the middle of the Souq, there are Indian, Moroccan, Persian, Iraqi, and Syrian restaurants. All have places to sit outside, and the area is lined with chairs, and in summer large standing fans sit behind some of them. There is an Arab shisha smoking area in the middle of the Souq, and one in the bazaar area. Shia is smoked in a pipe called a hookah. A wood base and long pipe, the smoker just sucks and puffs on it. There is a traditional Arab bazaar in the Souq where one can buy everything from gold and fabrics to toys, Arabic furniture, and souvenirs. These stalls are in long corridors with stone walls; some indoor, some outdoor. With the aroma of fresh spices; comingled with that of

were written in my villa on my compound in Doha, after a swim in a virtually empty pool in 40c Celsius or 104 Fahrenheit degree temperature. Both my diaries and reflections develop in length and depth as my trip goes on in time, particularly since the inspiration for the title *Just Keep Going, Man!* was inspired when I was somewhere in between Dunluce Castle and the town of Portrush, up the Causeway in Northern Ireland. Essentially in the middle of nowhere, I found an emotional uplift in a perfect stranger. So as the story gets philosophically deeper, so do my reflections. Also, the more friends I was reunited with, resulted in conversations about my current and past lives as an expat, and conversations about the political and economic state of the United Kingdom, all which are in my reflections. The voice in my logs does change after about the third week in my diaries as I pondered the thought of publication and thought I might be speaking to a wider audience, you my readers! I hope you enjoy the book and Just Keep Going, Man!

---

traditional Arab shisha smoking, and Arab incense called Bukhoor, the aroma is unique. Patrons truly get a smell, taste, and look of exotic Arabia. All are welcome at the Souq, with locals dressed in traditional clothes; the men in the thobe, a long white one-piece garment, with a white and red checkered head scarf; held down with a black rope head tie called an agal. Qatari women in the piece long black Abaya, but wear Western dress shoes, and all the fashionable ones. With Westerners and other Asians, some in jeans and T-shirts, the environment is a multicultural and harmonious one.

Dedicated to the People of Belfast

June 26, 2017 Edinburgh

Diaries: June 26. The first day of the month-long English tour has started. I changed my usual destination of Heathrow due to all the terrorist scares, and there was a British Airways strike, too, not that I am that afraid of a bomb going off, but I am put off by any hassle that makes travel uncomfortable and stressful. This time I flew into Edinburgh. Small airport, but a good decision; same system as Heathrow Airport for British passport holders. Machine operated; just a scan. Same for residents of Qatar. The United States is one of the few modern industrialized societies that still has immigration officers; many looking with scowls on their faces, asking their own citizens intimidating questions. I have a friend I met in Doha; both he and his wife are PhD holders. His wife is a constantly posting Facebook stuff, some very political and very liberal. If the post happens to be about police brutality or some racist happening, she might say in the post, "I am ashamed to be an American." I guess while recently traveling to the United States, just about a week ago, in fact, they stopped in Washington D.C., and her husband was pulled aside and asked some national security questions. I found out because she posted it. He is a white, highly educated male. In the post, she mentioned that they asked him who he knows in Doha. While there is a political embargo against Qatar, and it's claimed that this is due to Qatar having close ties with terrorists, does a clean-cut male, specs and all, traveling with a wife and two children, look like he is a threat to national security?

Reflections: Day One. I have many emotional connections in the United States, family and friends. Some of my childhood friends I have known for 34 years, and I care about them very deeply. During this trip, I kept in touch with family and friends through social media and phone calls. Of particular concern was a childhood friend that has been suffering from a very serious illness: urethra diverticulum. Just to give her a bit of moral support, I sent a few postcards and have been in touch with her while off the road. The above mindset of the immigration officer does suggest a slight paranoia. It's anyone who threatens harm or does acts of violence to anybody, American or non-, who should be the ones scrutinized and punished.

Reflections: Day One, continued. Past trips to Edinburgh: This was my fourth visit to Edinburgh in my lifetime. Before this trip, all were done before by train. Most major UK cities have train routes that reach Edinburgh. In the 1970s, there was one national railway, British Rail, but since privatization in the 1980s, various companies operate trains—Virgin Rail included. All of them operate similarly, with second- and first-class carriages. A buffet trolley goes up and down the aisle, full of sandwiches, usually ham and cheese, but spread from the sea or river, tuna or salmon, might be available. Coffee, beer, and soft drinks always are. The nuance of English class distinction remains; full meals are served in first class. Some carriers, such as Virgin, have leather seats in first class. A conductor collects all tickets on all trains, usually speaking in half sentences, saying, "Morning! Morning! Tickets, please." A polite "thank you very much" is said when the tickets are stamped and given back. It is a staple of "Englishness" that once was.

My first trip to Edinburgh was with my father when I was a junior in high school (aged 17, 1986). Then I visited again by myself in 1999. I was a director and part owner, with my father, of a nursing home in Kent. I took the train from London Kings Cross (about a four-train ride). The third trip was with my wife, Melissa, in 2011. We were staying with my mother's side of the family in Yorkshire. We had an overnight break in Newcastle, but our departure was from Wakefield Westgate. A good trip, but it ended on a devastating note, as I learned that my father had died on New Year's Eve in the United States. It's one of the only regrets in my lifetime that I was not with him that day.

So this was my first trip to Edinburgh Airport. After I had picked up my luggage off the belt, I caught a cab. In Edinburgh, the cabs are the same traditional black cab as in London. The box-shaped car has small front doors and big back doors on each side; and one long leather back seat. The Black Cab is a unique British landmark. My father's first job when we immigrated to the United States was at Redford Community Hospital, and his boss Dr. Curts, used to like going to London just for a Black Cab ride. However, just as London Black Cabs are expensive, so are the ones in Edinburgh the meter starts at 2 pounds 80 pence, and a several-mile journey is about 15 pounds (twenty US dollars). Thus, in London in the late 1980s and early 90s, the minicab was created. It's much cheaper for a long distance, usually a fixed charge. The Black Cab is good for a short distance.

I could hardly pronounce the name of the town I was going to, so when I got into the cab, I said, "Please take me to the Holiday Inn."

"Which one?" the cabbie replied. "There are three."

"The one in Coorforstein," I ventured, which gave it away to the cabbie that I had no clue of where I was going and most likely a tourist.

"Corstorphine?" he said.

"Yes."

It did not matter. The friendly conversation started as he drove past the beautiful scenery. In the far distance was one long mountain range, greenish with a tint of black, and clouds hovering over it with holes of blue sky. Just beautiful, really. I said just that, "Beautiful place."

He replied, "This is the best place in the world."

When we arrived at the hotel it was nothing extraordinary, although I did have a front room with the view of the mountain we passed. After a night flight I was tired, but curious about where I had to come to. Just like a little boy who thinks the moon is following him, the view of the mountain gave me good feelings of where I had come to.

Diaries: Day Two: June 27. Up this morning ridiculously early at 4:30 a.m., and have a little bit of jet lag and sleep deprivation. I just laid in bed for the next two hours. I thought nothing much would be open in this quaint, small, working class town. I bought a single bus ticket into the city center; and just after an area called Haymarket, I got off the bus. I was still tired and espied a Starbucks. I went in and ordered a cheese toasty and a large caramel macchiato. I sat down for ten minutes, and although it was ridiculously early, I was restless. I went to a window seat and just people watched. There were so many derelict types standing outside, smoking. I wondered what they were all doing up so early. I walked outside and noticed a Boots Pharmacy open. I needed some British paracetamol. They are much stronger than the kind that we get in Doha, but I decided to go to the pharmacy that was open across the street called Savers. They had paracetamol for just 19 pence. I took four packets to the counter, but the cashier at the counter told me under Scottish law I was only allowed to buy two, so I did.

Day Two Continued, June 27: Diaries. Reunited after more than two decades with Karen, who is a Scottish Law Scholar. *Scottish History1000-1707, Volume 1* by James Akaret is a book that she recommended to me when we met at Teuchters Bar. I got lost and went into another bar asking where the teachers bar is. The locals corrected me and said it's pronounced "tutors bar." I finally found it!!!

Day Two: Reflections: So why *are* all the derelict types up so early? Aren't they the ones supposed to be laying around in bed all day? On the bus I took into the city the driver said he did not have change. The bus I took one back to Corstorphine, it was a similar situation. I told the driver, "This must be for security purposes." He replied,"Ohhh, I," which means yes. With bus driver's not giving change and derelicts up early in the morning just loitering, I am inclined to think that there are issues of poverty and crime in Edinburgh, just as there are in most major European cities. I am hardly naïve, thanks to how much I have traveled, but my time in Doha has slightly removed me from my Western consciousness. In Doha there are no derelicts loitering anywhere. Might be a bit of reverse culture shock. So my Western consciousness was quickly coming back.

My reunion that evening with my Oxford summer term classmate Karen was a success. As one does when seeing an old friend, in the art of "catching up," we talked about her life as an academic and what I have been up to, which is usually long-winded, since I have lived in several different countries. Then, when her husband, James, joined us, the conversation turned to cities: Detroit's blight (which is due to residents moving out of inner-city Detroit and leaving buildings abandoned and falling into decay), how laid back the people of Edinburgh are, and the high energy of the city of London. The pub we went to was great. Wood floors and a long, wooden bar, with a great selection of Scotch whiskeys. The pub comes highly recommended. Then we went on to dinner at a French restaurant called appropriately Julez (my nickname, but I spell it Jules). Those who are very close to me and like to keep it real usually call me by this name. Anyway, the French restaurant in a lower ground floor had a vibrant and carefree atmosphere, where conversations are heard but do not carry. Again, this one comes highly recommended. About ten pounds for a steak with a side of any potato. Many pubs in the United Kingdom serve a rump steak, but this was much better than any steaks I have had in pubs. By today's standards, it is a reasonable price for just about anywhere.

Diaries: Day Three, June 28. Took the four-hour train ride from Edinburgh to Inverness. This was my social media post that I posted from the train:

Goodbye to the great city of Edinburgh!!! The town of Corstorphine, where I stayed, had friendly locals who were welcoming to the solo traveler. The pub I posted a picture of was in the town, and I became a frequent visitor. I also quickly started the habit of warming up with a scotch and a beer. Most of all, it was great to be reunited with my classmate Karen Grundizen Baston, from my summer studies at Oxford University, which shall I just say was a long time ago. Karen is also from my home state of Michigan, and after Oxford she went on to earn her PhD from the University of Edinburgh. She is a legal scholar of Scottish law. Bittersweet goodbye!!!! On to the next city!!!!

Day Three: Diaries: June 29. Staying at the Penta Cross Hotel. It is right across from the train station. Very comfortable, large double room, much bigger than the room I stayed at in Edinburgh. This is a smaller hotel, but the staff are very friendly, and the breakfast buffet is very good. Inverness is a small town; the central city can be seen in about a day. People in Edinburgh were more cautious and careful. Slight reticence of Anglo culture. People from Inverness are not quite as reserved. I went to a local pub, and all the waitress serving me called me was "Dear" and "Love." The outskirts of the city are beautiful. Rolling hills, and there is a river that runs through the city. While waiting for my tour at the bus station, the tour operator came to the bus stand and asked if I was going to John o' Groats; probably as far North as one can go! I said, "No, I am going to the Isle of Skye." The tour company, Highland Experience Tours, set off at about 9:15 a.m. It was about a 15- or 16-seated bus. The day trip would be a ten-hour day tour, and it was estimated that we would be back in Inverness at 7 p.m. The tour bus drove for a good two hours through the Scottish highlands, which was just beautiful. Rolling hills. We then stopped at an inn for a tea break near the Cuillin mountain range. After another 30- to 40-minute drive, we were near the Isle of Skye. We stopped to take some pics with a large body of water in the backdrop, and one could see the Isle of Skye in the background. After another twenty minutes, we stopped at the central stopping point of the Cuillin Mountains. There were lots of tourists and tour guides, some dressed in traditional Scottish kilts, telling the history of the mountains.

Day Three: Reflections.

More about the wanderings of my first day in Inverness.

My hotel, the Penta Cross Hotel, was very conveniently located about a block away from the central train station. My first impression was the same as my last one: Very Good. Prompt friendly check-in. When I was checking in, I asked the receptionist about tours to get to the Isle of Skye and Loch Ness. Although I was directly speaking with the receptionist, another staff member became involved in the conversation and offered help. He recommended several tour companies as well as how I could get to Loch Ness. He said it would be cheaper by train or bus. (I believe he said there are no trains to the Isle of Sky; one can only reach Skye by tour or private taxi. I did not see a train station anywhere near there when I went, so it is probably correct.) Then as I entered my room, I found it was all modern décor, a large comfortable bed, and, as at all UK hotels, an electric kettle. This particular hotel had a good selection of teas and coffees, a large-screen TV on the wall, and the room was twice the size of the room I stayed at in Edinburgh. Breakfast was not included at the Holiday Inn in Edinburgh, but at the Penta Cross it was. They had a buffet breakfast with the usual dishes: eggs, bacon, fried tomatoes, and cereal. Just about every hotel in the UK has Weetabix, which is an oval-shaped piece of wheat. To eat it, you break it up, with the shreds falling like crushed pieces of hay into the bowl with milk. I remember my grandfather used to eat Weetabix for breakfast, and he lived to be 92. Maybe a health tip for us all.

After breakfast, as I usually do on the first day that I arrive in a new city, I just roamed around to get a feel of it. Then I went in the opposite direction of the city and ended up by the river, about 100 yards or more wide, and I could not see an end to the river. That is what sparked my curiosity; I felt as if I needed to find out where the river led. I saw two church towers in the distance, each apart from one another, with oak trees in full bloom in front. I did not think or plan. I just started to walk, not knowing how far the church was or even if it was worth visiting, or if that was where I was going. When I arrived at the church, it was very small. Two red brick towers. The windows had a dark tint. Not stained glass. They hardly gave me a welcoming feeling and did not spark my curiosity to go inside. Although late June, it was cold! I just had a brief look around the church grounds. The wind was brisk, and it felt hard-pressed, as if the wind was pushing me to go somewhere inside and warm. Only wearing a jean jacket and a sleeved shirt did not help. I took a quick U-turn and walked halfway back to where I had started from. Now my tour guide was Mother Nature. I was cold and needed to get warmed up. I found a pub. A local recommended the venison burger, so that's what I ordered, along with a half-pint of beer, no scotch with it. I took it easy.

I finished my meal and then walked back to my hotel. Then I noticed there were a couple of men's clothing stores nearby my hotel—one on the same side of the street and the other across the street. I went into the one on the same side. It was a relaxed environment with several men's suit jackets on boxes. I browsed. Then, after about ten minutes, I told the white-haired, slightly potbellied salesmen I would be back. I also had a look at the men's shop across the street, which was a bit more upscale, selling the famous Harris Tweed jackets. These are handwoven and made in Scotland, and more expensive. When I was a student in London, a close friend of mine named Robert, who was a mature student at age 50, once told me, "Be careful, not cheap with money." Words to live by. With all the financial up's and down's from growing up in the affluent suburb of Grosse Pointe Farms, Michigan, to nearly twenty-four years of expatriot apartment living, this I understand. So I went back to the store across the street and bought a jacket, as the salesmen made me an offer, and I could not refuse. I love making deals with street salesmen and women who are honest and considerate. Priced at 125 pounds, but offered for 110—a brown lamb's wool jacket with red and black strips. The interior has a lining of a reddish shiny velvet. A touch of class with tradition, and good for winter wear. I also engaged in some good conversation at the counter with all of the salesmen in the store, talking about Scotland, places to live in the UK, and Scottish history. I had started my book *Scotland and the Second World War*, and I impressed them when I told them that the town of Corstorphine was named after a soldier who fought in the Great War. I had come a long way so quickly from saying Coorforstein to the cab driver at Edinburgh airport. It is just one particular aspect about the UK that I am attracted to. These were men in everyday jobs, but they were exceptional. All of them had a bit of general knowledge and could engage in deeper conversation than just common daily small talk.

Day Four: Reflections. Additional information about The Isle of Sky and Loch Ness.

In a short picture book titled *The Isle of Skye*, which I purchased when I was actually at The Isle of Skye, it says, "It should begin with the Cuillin." As I mentioned in my diaries, the central meeting place of the Cuillins has a quintessential stream cascading over rocks. I posted a pic of it on social media, and the reactions I got were that it was just spectacular. It was. The tour bus took us to The Isle of Skye. It is a small fishing town with a few pubs and restaurants and souvenir shops. It was overrun with tourists when I went, and I have to say I was put off. The tour guide gave us one hour to spend there, so instead of going to a sit-down restaurant, I bought fish and chips to go at a shop right on the pier, and ate them there.

The last stop on the tour was Urquhart Castle at Loch Ness, but just for a five-minute picture-taking session. As we drove past the loch, one can tell that it is very deep. The water stacks very high against the land. It is no kidney-shaped type of lake, like in many lakes in my home state of Michigan. After eight hours on a bus, I could hardly walk due to my physical injury, and it was pouring down rain, so I stayed on the bus. It is a pretty spooky place. It was raining, black and grey, not even a tint of blue sky anywhere. After the five minutes was up, most of the tourists got back on the bus.

The guide showed us the famous black-and-white "surgeon's photograph" of the Loch Ness Monster taken by Robert Kenneth Wilson. The original picture is just a hoax. The guide told us the man who took it was some pauper-type drifter. What is amazing is that this legend was believed for years afterwards, and there was an organized search for the monster in the 1960s. I even remember my family in Yorkshire saying that the loch goes out to sea and that there might be more of sea creatures. Loch Ness is also the place where the infamous occultist Aleister Crowley owned a home. Several British musicians took an interest in him. Ozzy Osbourne wrote a song about Crowley, and the guide mentioned that the guitarist Jimmy Page bought his home and lived there for just seven days. According to the guide there is a scene in the movie *The Song Remains the Same* with Jimmy page at the home. There is a direct train to Loch Ness from Inverness Station, with hotels and shops in the area. One can explore on their own if they like, but just be sure to keep a watch out for Nessie, as some believe she still roams the loch.

Day Five: June 30, Diaries. Logging the miles of my trip. 3,000 miles to Edinburgh from Doha. Edinburgh to Inverness, 155. And yesterday I did 360 miles to the Isle of

Skye and back. My inquiries about getting to Broadie Castle have not been successful. There are no trains there or even buses. With all the walking I have done, my body is beginning to ache, and I am tired. Each day I have posted on social media. And just to have some fun, I have titled each post Captain's Log. The character Captain James Kirk used to say this at the end of the original *Star Trek* series. This is the social media post written on the way to Glasgow:

Goodbye Inverness!!!! A small and some might call it even a sleepy town. However, it is close to Loch Ness, the Isle of Skye, and if one wants to go to the top of Scotland, one can go to Wick or John O Groats. Past that is Kirkwell and Skara Brae. For serious readers like myself Inverness does have a well-established book shop called Leakey's, and it's all second hand, but not second-hand priced. There are bargain charity shops for the potluck reader, and WHSmiths, the main section of which, it should come as no surprise, was dedicated to Scottish history. I bought *Flowers of the Forest, Scotland and the First World War*. There are memorials dedicated to soldiers that gave their lives in the Great War. As one of my former professors mentioned in a recent post, the Great War is a historical event whose repercussions we are still living with. One hundred years later, the Middle East is still unsettled. I had great conversations with some locals and was told by the hotel receptionist, "Come back in winter. It won't be so busy, and you will have more peace and quiet." Maybe, although I just might need another three layers of clothing!

Detour on the tour as I now move on to Glasgow and soon hope to be reunited with another good friend.

Day Five: Reflections. I was sorry I did not get a chance to see Brodie Castle in Inverness, as there is no public transportation to it. I asked several locals about it. One can only get there by taxi. It's a white Tudor castle that the exterior front has ten medium-sized windows and nine large ones with small oval towers on top of it. The sixteenth century castle is decorated elegantly with many English and Dutch paintings. It's about 25 miles east of Inverness.

Day Six: July 1, Diaries. I Arrived in Glasgow. Miles from Inverness: 168. At first when I arrived at Queens Train Station, I looked for the taxi stand but did not see one. I asked a police officer where the taxi stand is, and he directed me straight out of the station and then left. I followed his instructions, but I found no taxis. I started walking and found that other individuals were in the same situation. I did manage to hail a cab and make it to my hotel.

The city was much more crowded than the sleepy town of Inverness. Some areas looked run down, and there were beggars and more of the "downtrodden." I had a slight uncomfortable feeling that my hotel might be in a neighborhood that might be unsafe. It was an older hotel. The receptionist looked tired, with bags under her eyes, and I told her I had a booking. She said, "Do you? Check in time is 2:00 p.m."

Day Six: Reflections. The name of hotel I stayed at in Glasgow was the Alexander Thomson Hotel. My first impression as I approached the hotel was slightly negative, as there is a pellet gun store next to it and a sexy lingerie store. The hotel is slightly run down inside. Then when the clerk, bleach blonde and middle aged, unsmiling and tired looking, abruptly said, "Check in time is 2:00 p.m.," I thought I might have made a mistake by booking the hotel. I went upstairs to a lounge area, which had a shelf of old books, a red leather sofa, and old curtains hanging in the windows. I just parked myself on a chair. Then I saw a man behind a counter adjacent next to the lounge. I was very tired and really wanted to check into my room. I asked the man if I could, and he quickly picked up the phone and asked the clerk at the front counter if there was a room available. She told him yes, and he said that I booked a basic room, but that if I was willing to pay for an upgrade, I could check in immediately, so I took the upgrade.

The hotel is on Argyle Street, close to central station. The next morning, when I went to have breakfast, the buffet had about a dozen or so dishes to choose from. The breakfast room and was packed full of guests, but the staff moved at a fast pace, and I could tell had a strong work ethic. Never judge a book by its cover, I reminded myself, picking through the sausages, eggs, breads, and cereals. I would stay at the Alexander Thomson Hotel again.

My touring time in Newcastle was short and sweet. I went to the Gallery of Modern Art; one that has a well-known landmark outside of it, a bronze statue of the Duke of Wellington, one of the officers who fought and helped defeat Napoleon at Waterloo. The statue has an orange-and-white fire cone on top of it—a bit of rebellion there and a touch of anti-English statement? Similar to love, art lies in the heart and eyes of the beholder.

Day Seven: July 2, Diaries. Glasgow to Newcastle: miles 151.Total miles in a week 3,834. Getting past the initial stigma of the city, I found the people of Glasgow very friendly. I have to say at first I was intimidated, but I had a conversation with a middle-aged man from Sterling. He started the conversation, and after a bit of introduction, he said, "Scotland is good, isn't it?" I told him about my father being from the tribe of Pashtuns. I found Scots to be the same: warm and friendly, but strong. Same as the Pashtuns. Best friend but worst enemy. I told him "I'm glad I did not piss anybody off!"

Day Eight: July 3, Diaries. It was good to catch up with my friend Helen Higgins last night. We worked together at Berlitz Language School in Istanbul. However, going out to find a decent breakfast in Newcastle was hard work; I am not really feeling the vibe of the city. People looked like they did not want to get out of bed on a Monday morning, and there was a depressive mood in the air. Found a diamond in the rough when I went out in the afternoon: the literary and philosophical society of Newcastle. Good library of books; made a donation.

Day Eight: Reflections. I arrived in Istanbul in 2008. I met Helen there. She was thin as a pencil, with long straight brown hair, usually in a ponytail. She has a nature as good as gold, and a touch of motherly love in her. I felt an emotional connection. Being brought up by my father, I grew up without my mother. So motherly love is something I have always needed and have unconsciously gravitated to. Helen and I also had something in common: we both were from the North of England. However, being a third culture kid, one can't tell my background. I sound North American, so she like most people was surprised when I shared my West Yorkshire birthright. Another teacher from Manchester joined the emotional chain, and then there were three. His name is Paul. Helen's sister Judith came to Istanbul about six months after I did, and she also joined the fray. We lived in the suburb of Kozytagi, pronounced Kozata, on the Asian side of Istanbul. Istanbul has a unique geographical distinction of two separate sides. One called The Asian and the other called the European. The Bosphorus strait, which separates the two sides, has frequent ferries crosses from Kadikoy on the Asian side to Eminou on the European. It's one of the unique aspects about Istanbul. The ferry crossing gives it a small fishing town feel in a city that has a population of 15 million. Helen and I would eat lunch with other teachers at a kebab restaurant on the suburban street we lived on. Helen organized many lunches, get-togethers, and nights on the town. One of Helen's favorite past times is salsa dancing. Helen, Judith, and I and a few other teachers grooved it up in a nightclub next to Febeerbacha football stadium in Kadikoy one night. The most memorable night occurred because Helen's birthday is close to mine. We organized a joint birthday party at my apartment, which I shared with two other teachers. It turned into a full-fledged drunken dance party with me playing some of my CDs, everything from pop 80s and 90s groups, the B52s to Oasis. About twelve teachers were bopping up and down in my living room. Ahh, youth....... Helen, Paul, and

Judith would leave one year before I left Istanbul. I was lost. I went into a mental downward spiral, due to severe isolation and a tainted love affair, but that's another story….. Ahh, youth……

So nine years later… I met her and her boyfriend, Richard, in the lobby of my hotel at 7:00 p.m. We took a walk to the castle in the middle of the city center, hence the name Newcastle. We stood in front of the castle and took a few pics. There is a large river in Newcastle called the Tyne. We walked along the pier in front of the river. There are a few restaurants and pubs along it. It was a sunny beautiful summer day, with the shining, I walked along in a slow stride, looking cool wearing my sun sunglasses, but then suddenly, there was pain all over my body. I had overdone it. I did not say anything for about ten minutes, but finally I said, "Helen, I am in pain." She did not quite seem to understand. The last time she had seen me was nine years ago, when I was in tip-top physical condition. Ten minutes later, I could not walk at all. She asked what we should do. I said, "Take me to the nearest pub." "The nearest pub?" she replied. "Yes." She and Richard took me to The Red House, which is a small tavern with wooden beams—nice, really. I ordered a scotch and a beer and had a good rest for an hour, and I was cured!!

Day Nine: July 4, Diaries: A damp, rainy day, but it's my friend James' birthday today. I sent him a birthday message, and he is coming to of all places Newcastle!! Hope to meet up later. I posted on social media, wishing my childhood friends in my home state of Michigan in the United States a happy Fourth of July. Today is a damp, miserable day. I finally found a small, cozy watering hole to have a drink in, called The Box. I had two great on tap beers: Gipsy Hill, brewed in South London, and Northern Monk, from Yorkshire. There was no food served at The Box, so the chap at the bar recommended that I go to the waiting room across from the train station. It is a big pub with modern décor, and everything is brand new. It even smells new. Now drinking Hop House. I wondered why some folk seemed depressed in Newcastle: as I look out the window, after I have moaned and groaned about the weather, I see a young man covered in a green blanket sitting in the rain. That's why some people are depressed-poverty.

Day Nine: Reflections: After six years of living in Qatar, I was not used to seeing beggars. There are none in Qatar, but there were many in Newcastle, compared to other cities I went to. I'm not sure why. Newcastle is a very industrial city, and over the years the public sector has been reduced dramatically in the United Kingdom, everything from free legal aid to money for education, even money for the disabled. All public sector funding has been dramatically reduced.

Day Ten: July 5, Diaries. Last night was a nice evening. Helen and Richard had invited me around for a meal. They live a ten-minute walk past the train station, in a top-floor flat. I chatted awhile with Helen and told her about the trip I took with my dad in 1989 to Gilgit, Pakistan, we drove from Islamabad on the Karakorum highway that Marco Polo once traveled on. I was getting altitude sickness after I would eat oranges. I also told her about my father being in the Hashim Khan movie *Keep Eye on Ball*. We searched online for the trailer to the film, but were unsuccessful in finding it. As we gabbed away, her partner, Richard, cooked pasta for us. When he was finished cooking, we had a well-rounded discussion; I did lead most of it, about some of the intellectual topics that have been on my mind recently, such as why most of my close friends are Catholic. I mentioned James' name and Richard googled it. An article came up that said James wrote when he worked at Citizens Advice Bureau, which is a UK Charity organization offering free legal advice. Although James had said, he was coming up to Newcastle for a political conference on his birthday, in his true eccentric fashion he missed his stop and ended up in Leeds!

Reflections: Day Ten. When I was seventeen, my father, my brother Nick, and I flew from Detroit to Islamabad, Pakistan, nearly a day's journey with layovers in Paris and Cairo. My father's brother, Kamal, was waiting at the airport to greet us with his daughter, who couldn't have been more than five years old, a driver, and a guide. The seven of us drove in a compact Suzuki jeep to Gilgit. A part of the word that several famous men in history have traveled to, Alexander the Great and Marco Polo. Gilgit is close to China and near the Hunza Valley. Alexander the great invaded the Hunza valley in 325 B.C, and some villagers who live in this area consider themselves descendants of him. Unlike Pakistan's who usually have brown eyes and dark hair one might see blonde hair and blue eyes.[2] The 288-mile journey started out on a freeway

---

[2] This information about the Hunzel Valley comes from the book The Karakoram Highway and the Hunza Valley, 1998, (p. 7) by Annette Braker and Horst H Geerken. This couple took a similar journey that my father, Nick and I did. They also started their travels in Islamabad on the Grand Truck railroad then on to the Karakoram Highway. They spent time in the Hunza Valley which is North of Gilgit, and then they traveled on into China.

(or motorway, as it's called in the UK), and on the Grand Trunk railroad,[3] but then we drove through the rugged terrain of some of the highest mountains in the world (some 8,000 meters high) on the Karakorum highway, it boarders Kashmir and is the road that Marco Polo once traveled on. [4] To say the least, it was a turbulent, petrifying, but spectacular journey. We drove through waterfalls, but there were no guard rails on the thin dirt roads. It was a long look down. Most of the road was one way, but was being used as a two-way by buses traveling with passengers. The memory that resonates in my mind is meeting an oncoming bus, which was decorated orange; I vividly see in my memory splashes of white on it and writing what must have been in Urdu. I remember the bus coming straight at us and our driver pulling to the nearest open spot he could find. However primitive the means of travel and road we took, it was civilized and skillful driving. I was hungry, and my father fed me oranges. As we drove higher up, I got altitude sickness. Out came the oranges. My father, the ever tender, loving physician and dad that he was, cajoled and nursed me through my sickness.

---

[3] The Grand Trunk railroad is one Asia oldest roads, built before the birth of Buddha, it has connected central and South Asia since. https://en.wikipedia.org/wiki/Grand_Trunk_Road

[4] Marco Polo was one of the first adventures to travel extensively throughout Asia. His journey started in Italy in 1271, and lasted 24 years. He wrote a book about it, simply titled, Marco Polo The Travels, known as one of the greatest travel books ever written, it reads like a history book. Marco Polo gives detailed account of people he met and how they lived. On his travels along the Karakorum, he observed that the men were permitted to have multiple wives, and up to a 100. As he describes "if he has wherewithal to maintain them". (P71). He mentions leaving the Karakorum and traveling to a place called Bargu, and the staple daily diet of the peoples there: reindeer, fish, and no alcohol.(p76)

I have often pondered why most of closet friends are Catholic. There is a strong tradition of education in the Catholic Church, and most of my friends who are Catholic have a strong desire to learn, just as I do. As a people, the Catholics, especially the Irish Catholics, have suffered religious persecution. Is there a passed-down mentality of empathy and understanding for what it's like to be a minority? Perhaps it is just a matter of circumstance.

Day Ten, Continued: July 5, Diaries. This is a Facebook post of day-trip to London: Captain's Log, Tour Day Ten:

> Went on a day trip to Paddington, London. Had a laid-back day in my old neighborhood of Paddington. I got a haircut, bought two more books (11, now), and sunbathed in Hyde Park. London was my sixth city in ten days, and I have traveled 1,500 miles in one week. However, travel is not called adventure for nothing. Going down to London I felt terrible. In Qatar it is standard practice for me to drin ten glasses of water a day, but in the UK, I am guessing residents drink much less. It's more like cups of tea and coffee, same in the United States. Of course Americans keep the soft drink companies in business by consuming lots of soda pop. Anyway, I was terribly dehydrated and had a cup of tea and several bottles of water. By the time I reached London, I felt better. The high energy of London perked me up, too, although I did encounter a rude incident with an impatient traveler not wanting to wait in the queue for a London underground ticket, but that's the big city, and I just ignore that aspect of it. The train back to Newcastle that evening was

going so fast that plates and cups would shake when we passed another train. "Are we on the *Titanic*?" I asked the other passengers. I told one of the staff that I was going to be seasick! The staff took a shine to me, and the scotch kept coming. With my fresh haircut and laid-back American jean jacket, I was dressed to impress. A few stops before Newcastle, one of the passengers comes up to me and said, "I know who you are! You're Pete Sampras!!!" All this excitement caused me get off on the wrong stop, but then I got back on the train and finally made it to Newcastle.

Day11: July 6: Diaries I caught up with another old friend, Rachel Arckley. We taught English together in South Korea. We went to the restaurant *Pleased to Meet You.* It features an old-style painted wall that looks like one of those canopies with nineteenth century type of art painted on it. Great food for a reasonable price, and an ever-so-genteel waitress. I ordered an IPA, but the waitress told me the bar was out of it. "We have another IPA," she said, "but the name is ...well...." "Yes?" I asked. "Screaming Bitch," she said, blushing.

Day 11: Reflections: Rachel and I worked in Seoul, South Korea, at an after-school called Sogang Language School, from 2005 to 2006. It was also a reunion after a long time. We had been in touch via social media, just as Helen and I had, but distance had kept us apart. Rachel reminded me that we had lived in the same apartment building provided by the school, called "The Happy House." Rachel lived downstairs, and I had an upstairs flat. Although we lived in The Happy House, I am not sure if it was the happiest time of my life. It was the first country I had lived in as an adult, outside of the United States and Britain. It was the first time I had no friends and family around.

The reasons for my disgruntled feelings were: first, the winters are really cold in Korea, and the summers are very hot. Back then, I worked out about three times a week, so I was in good shape, but ironically not as good as today, as I work out now every day. As soon as I got there, I was ill, and I was unprepared to handle it. The school sent me I to a teachers training course at one of the major universities in Seoul. I only had a long sleeve shirt on, and it poured down rain that day. I listened to one lecture and just blew the rest of the day off. When the school found out about this, it was if I had committed some grave sin. The director came looking for me at my apartment! He rang the doorbell about eight times. I blew that off too. I saw him the next day. He was pretty nice about it, but he said if I was sick they would take me to a doctor. I was not that sick, really, but ended up ill many times after that. I took myself to the doctor. Even getting sick for real caused problems between myself and the school. My stint in my first foreign country was not that long; I ended up quitting after six months. However, the goodbye party was a blast. All eight foreign teachers, as we were called, attended. We went to a Korean restaurant and then to a bar. When most of the teachers went home, Rachel and I and a teacher named Nathan went to an afterhours bar until 3 a.m.

It was a short-lived professional experience, and I still remember calling my brother Nick in the United States and telling him that I quit. "Where will you go now?" he asked. Luckily, my cousin Umar, who had left Peshawar,

Pakistan, at eighteen, he had established an auto company in Tokyo, Japan, that sold used cars, in developing parts of the globe. The Africa market was the biggest exporter for his cars. So I went there. Later I was sent on assignment to the Dominican Republic, but that's another story.... Anyway, it was good to be reunited with Rachel, and I am sure our friendship will last for many years more than my time in Korea did.

Day 12: July7, Diaries: It was time to leave Newcastle, and I warmed up to it. People were much more conservative than in Scotland. Most of the staff at the Royal Station hotel where I was staying called me "Sir." None of the staff in Scotland did. Checkout time was also earlier than in Scotland: 11:00 a.m. My flight was a late afternoon one, so I had plenty of time. Breakfast was not included with my room, which was good, really. Breakfast at three- and four-star hotels in England usually 10 to 15 pounds overpriced. Most UK cities have small cafes or pubs to get the same style English breakfast for much less. I found one right across from my hotel and had a vegetarian breakfast. My flight was not until 4:30 p.m., so I had plenty of time. However, once my time in the city I am visiting is over, I leave. Why waste time? On to the next destination.

I went back to my hotel, collected my luggage, and caught a taxi to the airport. There was a taxi stand right in front of hotel, so I was on to my next city, Belfast. At least so I thought. Newcastle Airport was small. Just one building. I had plenty of time, so I bought a cup of tea and finished up the current book I was reading, *The Holocaust: A New History* by Laurence Rees. On the cover page it's called a

33

masterpiece by Andrew Roberts, whoever that might be. The book is a fantastic one. It's a sensitive and serious subject, which I have taken so, since I started reading about it in college. I have read many books on the Holocaust, taken a class on Coursera on it, through University of California Irvine, (the class was co-taught by a Holocaust survivor), and I have visited two concentration camps, Sachsenhausen in Oranienburg, Germany, 22 miles north of Berlin, and Dachau, about 12 miles northwest of Munich. I learned tangibles that I never knew, such as the Final Solution and systematic destruction of European Jewry that started when the Nazis invaded Poland. I highly recommend the book.

I checked in several hours early, and had joined British Airways executive club, so I avoided the long queue of economy class. I just had a brief window shop and was walking towards my gate when saw the BA executive lounge. Having just joined executive club, I did not think I would be able to use it. I went into the lounge and said just that, but I saw that BA is part of One World Alliance, which has reciprocal arrangements with about a half dozen carriers. I was a member of the Qatar Airways program and I knew my number by heart. I presented it, and I was in. I read my book, had a couple of rum and cokes, and boarded my plane. I had a connecting flight at Heathrow in London. The flight to Heathrow would put 1,750 UK miles traveled.

After all passengers had boarded, we were ready for takeoff. However, ten minutes passed, then twenty. The captain said we were waiting for the small runway to clear and it should just be a few more minutes. By then it was half an hour late, and there was another problem. There was a hole in the runway! And the plane could not take off!! Well, an hour passed and the plane finally took off!! Standard usual apologies for the delay by the captain.

We landed an hour later, and I started a conversation, with a calm brunette from Australia. I said, "It should be no problem. I can make my next flight." Just before landing, one of the flight crew, announced that several of the passengers had connecting flights and that their dedicated team of customer service professionals would be happy to answer any questions about connecting ones. Usually relaxed and never in a hurry to get off the plane, I made a mad dash. I asked a BA representative about my flight as soon as I got off the plane, but she had no clue. I carried on to connecting flights. I looked up and down the connecting flights screen, but Belfast could not be found. There was a customer service section, but there was a long line. I stood in the line (called a queue in the UK) for connecting flights anyway. When it got to my turn, the attendant said, "Your flight is not in this terminal." I said, "Where is it, then?" "I have no idea," she said, shaking her head. Flustered, I took down a strip of a divider. The attendant, who like myself looked to be British Asian, but female, attractive with dark long hair and brown eyes that turned bloodshot red, got up from her seat and said, "Do you know this is a restricted security area!!! Do you want me to make you understand that?!" I declined her offer and stood in the customer service line. I knew I would miss my flight. I was one of the last in line to get to the counter. I was very relaxed. The customer service agent told me that I had missed my flight, but she would search for another one. She said, "We have a flight at 7:20 in the morning." I said, "It is not that urgent. I am going to visit a friend in Belfast, and I have been through this before. This happened to me in 2000, when I was coming back from Greece." She said, "You sure do have a good memory." While she searched, I excused myself and went to the bathroom. I passed through the restricted security area, and the agent who threatened me now would not even make eye contact with me. She had moved on. When I returned, the middle-aged agent with short, blonde hair, serious, kind, with a wedding ring on, said, "I can book you on a flight at 11:20 a.m." I said, "That is fine." She said, "We will put you up in a hotel and pay for your dinner and breakfast." The hotel was the same one I am supposed to return to when I get back to London. By now there were no customers in line for connecting flights. The other agent, a young brunette with a cute countenance of youth, said, "You will be able to test it out." The other agent, Rachel, continued with my booking, checked my one bag in for the next day, and gave me my vouchers with an overnight kit.

I went to find the bus for my hotel, the Hotel Mercure. I also had a voucher for the bus. At the hotel, I showed my voucher and said, "I am checking in compliments of British airways." The first thing I did was check Facebook to contact my friend Robert. His Facebook message said he was on the way to the airport. I sent a message that I had missed my flight and I would be arriving the next day. Then opened up my overnight kit. It had a white T-shirt, small tube of toothpaste—and I mean small, the size of a finger nail—deodorant the size of a small, round nail polish bottle, a razor, and must have had shaving cream, but never took any notice since I have my own. The kit given to me in 2000 had white cotton underpants, but things have changed; none with this kit. I then went down to dinner and the restaurant bar. I proceeded to order from the standard menu, but when I showed the waitress my voucher, she then pulled out a different menu from behind the bar. It had three courses on it. I ordered the soup, tomato with beef. The waitress, with specs, dark skin, and an accent not from the UK, said, "It's excellent. Everybody says it's excellent." I ordered chicken and had my favorite sticky toffee pudding. Anywhere that I had dessert in the UK, I ordered sticky toffee pudding. All this and a large glass of white wine, which was not compliments of BA, was fantastic!! However, when I returned to my room and checked my Facebook messages, my friend asked if I could take a bus to his house. I was tired, and really this was about the last hassle I needed. I asked how much it would cost to get to his house by cab. He said not cheap: 70 pounds. I told him I would think about what to do. He mentioned he had been traveling for two weeks and needed to catch up on sleep. I returned the message and told him to get some rest, traveling from Toronto is a long way. I thought about it and was just going to stay in London, but since the agent booked my luggage on the next flight, I had to go. I booked two nights at a Ramada Inn on booking.com and I went to bed.

Day 13: July 8, Diaries. I skipped breakfast and went to Heathrow in the morning on the hotel shuttle. I already had my boarding pass, so I went straight through to security. The environment at Heathrow terminal five was very relaxed. I went through security, and the guard after the metal detector was another attractive British Asian. I made a joke, telling her, "I thought it was going to be my lucky day and I was going to get patted down." She laughed. I shopped for a bit. I clearly did not need any more books, but I found a toy train for my son, Kasey. I had a cup of tea and continued to read my book on the Holocaust. After I was finished, I went near the gate. I tried to go to the BA executive lounge, but this time I did not have such a welcoming attendant. I gave her my Qatar Airways number, but she said I was ruby status and not allowed to use the lounge. My flight boarded soon anyway. I took my seat and soon was on my way to Belfast!!! The flight to Belfast was 468 miles. I now had traveled 2,228 UK miles.

When I got to Belfast, I waited for my luggage and after some time, I sat down. My luggage had been lost twice before, so I was prepared!! Before even the last bag came on, I went to luggage claim and told the attendant my situation. She said, "Can I have your luggage tag please?" She scanned it and said, "Your luggage is still at Heathrow." She took the address of the hotel I was staying in and gave me another overnight kit. I took a taxi to my hotel from George Best Belfast City Airport for about ten pounds. It was cold that day, and with no clothes but the ones I was wearing, I put both undershirts on. I felt like the character "The Fonz" played by Henry Winkler in the 1970s television show *Happy Days*.

I did not have my luggage, I was staying at a hotel, not with my friend, but I thought, "the show must go on." I had on two undershirts and a suit jacket. It must have only been 18 Celsius that day, but with two undershirts, it was not so bad! There was a leaflet about a Belfast Mural Taxi Tour for 35 pounds. I told the boy behind the desk that I would have a think about it. I then sent off about 10:00 am and went then to the city center which was only about fifteen minutes from my hotel. I went to Burger King and ate some junk. There is a bookstore in Belfast called Seasons. I bought book number twelve for just 2 pounds, 99 pence, *Nowhere's Child* by Kari Rosvall. The cover reads, "The inspiring story of how one women survived Hitler's breeding camps and found an Irish home." I went to tourist information and found a leaflet about a place I really wanted to go: Dunluce Castle. After going to tourist information, I was tired and went back to the hotel, but on the way back I saw a jazz club called Bert's. I went in and made a reservation for Sunday. When I returned to my hotel that evening I went to have a drink at the hotel bar. I ordered a rum and coke. There was a two-man band playing—one with a guitar and one on piano. I sat down and intensely listened to the music for a good half an hour before the band stopped for the evening.

Day 14: July 9, Diaries. My luggage still had not arrived, but I had breakfast and went for a wander around town. There was a hop-on, hop-off tourist type bus on the high street in the city center. I asked how much it was, and the attendant said 12 pounds, 50 fifty pence. I thought to myself, *this really is not too bad.* Hop-on, hop-off are usually double the price in London. I got on the bus, and one of the first stops was an exhibit about the *Titanic.* I did not get off the bus, but thinking about it, the ship must have started from here. A lot of people, most of them, got off the bus. I found the next stop much more interesting. It was the Irish Parliament building. It stood back on a hill with shiny green grass in front. I got off the bus. It was a grim dark day, and there were only a couple of tourists walking around. Took a few pics and walked around the grounds. I was finished in about 15 minutes. I sat on a bench and started talking to a middle-aged women. As I started to talk to her, it started to rain. She said she was a nurse by trade and worked during the time of The Troubles. I think she was older than middle aged. She said, "9/11 was a tragedy but most people did not know anybody who died, in the time of The Troubles, everybody knew someone that died." Maybe this was too deep a conversation with a stranger as she excused herself, saying she had a bingo game to get to. The rain continued, and I was wearing only my suit jacket. I went to go wait for the bus. The hop-on, hop-off stops at the murals, and I was interested. The bus came after about 15 minutes. The next stop was Freedom Corner. The Unionist area of Belfast with murals painted on buildings and walls by those who support the British government. The area I am guessing is predominately Protestant and is in East Belfast. As I got off the bus, the driver wished me the best. There were small Union Jacks hung in a row from lamps and on poles outside homes. This type of overt patriotism is never displayed in England. Only when there is something like a Queen's Jubilee celebration are so many flags hung up. I checked out a few murals and took pictures of them. It was Sunday, and the area was back in time; most shops where shut. Most of the men walking streets wore jeans or track suits, and most smoked. It took me about half an hour to take about twenty pictures. I waited at the stand for the next hop-on, hop-off bus. A group of about ten men walked towards me, and I felt intimidated. I pulled myself back, they passed, and it was fine. I waited for my bus, and a young family came to the stand. As I looked at my pictures, a hop-on hop-off bus passed. I said "There goes my bus!" The young man from the family said that was a tourist bus. Wearing my suit jacket and with no camera hanging from my neck, I must have blended in. I waited another 20 minutes. The family caught their bus, and I still waited. About 15 minutes later, I saw a hop-on hop-off bus. Instead of waiting, I panicked and started to run towards it. As I got towards it, it was not my tour, then my bus passed!!! I got on the other bus that was not my tour I told the driver it was not my bus, but begged and pleaded to buy a ticket. He said that I could not sell me one, and I sat down. As we neared the city center, there were not many passengers on the bus, so I walked up to stand next to him. We started talking, and I told him what happened. He said, "I am from a Unionist area myself, but getting stuck in East Belfast! There are some 'nutters' down there!" We got to the city center, and I said after this experience, I could use a drink. We passed a pub called Hercules. I said, "What about that one?" He said, "This is a Catholic area, and it is a Catholic pub." I said nothing, I was out of my comfort zone and had to go with whatever happened. He dropped me off and charged me nothing.

I went back to my hotel and asked about my luggage. It had arrived, just like a long lost friend. I eagerly took it upstairs and unpacked. I rested for a while and then, around seven, showered and got dressed up, putting on my grey, white and charcoal checkered slacks that I had bought in Rome, and keeping the grey jacket on. My reservation at a jazz club was not until 8 p.m., so I had time to kill. I walked around a bit and a few minutes before my reservation, I went in. I was escorted to my table and sat down. The jazz music did not come on until 9, so I took my time. I first started with some sweet-and-sour gin drink. The waiter kindly brought me an *Irish Times*. I then ordered a three-course meal. For starter, I ordered crab salad, then leek, and fish for my main. The meal was fair. The crab salad was a spread with toast. The fish was okay, and so was the music, but the price for all was 30 pounds, which for a place like that in the UK is reasonable. It was a memorable day and a nice evening.

Day 15: Reflections. Just to give an idea of how much traveling I have done, this is the third time I have arrived in a UK airport but my luggage has not. The first was in 2000. I ran a family-owned nursing home in Kent. I solemnly closed it in a month, and sold it in a week. With no job and no place to go, one of my former male nurses encouraged me to go on holiday. I flew from London Heathrow to Athens, Greece, for a few days and then on to Crete. When I returned to Athens from Crete, my bags were not there, but I went on to catch my connecting flight to Heathrow. Same procedure. I was given an overnight kit—this one had underpants in it—and put up in a hotel. That same evening, or it might have been the next evening, a representative brought my luggage up to my room. I worked for my cousin Umar in the Dominican Republic, and although very well paid at $5,000 dollars for a few days per months' work, after eight months, I quit. I flew Air France from Santo Domingo to London Heathrow. I had one big crate and a large suitcase. Neither arrived. As I always used to do, I gave my grandmother a ring and then just showed up on her doorstep. So did my bags a few days later!

Day 15: July 10, Diaries. Tired that morning, I had got up in the middle of the night again. I probably was not quite settled yet, and although my bed was comfortable, it had a cold feel to it. With the more modest hotels in the UK, the heat is only turned on at night. I called reception to ask about the heat, and it was turned on at 10 p.m. and then again at 7 a.m. The attendant I talked to was nice and showed concern, saying, "Make sure your heat is turned on." This is a very modest attempt to control the temperature. It usually drives Americans mad. I went through this when I was a student in England, so I am used to it. I took the high ground and just thanked the gentlemen I spoke to. I got up and pressed "on."

When I spoke to a lady at tourist information, she said I could walk to West Belfast to see what is called "Murals," "the Republican ones," such as the Bobby Sands mural and what she called "the peace wall." So off I went. I did have to ask a couple of times where West Belfast is, but I made it. Unlike the murals in East Belfast, in West Belfast there is one wall, and this is what the representative must have meant by calling it "the peace wall." Unlike East Belfast, it did not have as strong, coarse feel. After I took my pictures of the murals, I went up the road, and just as in East Belfast, almost all the males had on jeans or track suits and were smoking, and this is on a working day. Although different areas that hold two different political views and two different sects of Christianity, they share a social class in common—working class. I walked further up the road and saw a sign on a shop that said Sinn Féin. I went in and it was just that, a Sinn Féin book and souvenir shop. I had to ring the doorbell, and an old, grey-haired lady opened the door. I am a born Englishmen, but kept objective. I looked around, as there were books by Gerry Adams and souvenir placemats with guys with masks on that said IRA. I hardly was going to buy a Gerry Adams book, but I did find a book about The Troubles called *Down North:*

Reflections of Ballymurphy and the Early Troubles by Ciarán De Baróid. I have not started reading it yet, but hopefully, by keeping an open mind, I might learn something. I paid for my book and left the store. I was very thirsty by this time and hungry. I looked for a pub in the heart of West Belfast, but again felt intimidated. There where men standing outside pubs, smoking. I kept moving on and finally mustered up the courage to go into a pub. I said to the bar man, who looked hard and with a scowl of his face, "You alright? Are you serving any food here?" The scowl came off his face, and he said, "Not here, but up the road." Well, I never found up the road. I did see more chain commercial pubs, but again they had men smoking outside of them, and I was intimidated. I kept moving on until I got back to the center of town. I searched for a bit and then went to the pub that the bus driver mentioned was a Catholic pub, The Hercules. It had a restaurant upstairs and was calm, quiet, and peaceful. I ordered a fish and chips and a lager beer. I recommend the pub. I had done several hours walking and was tired. I went back to my hotel for the rest of the day.

Day 16: July 11, Diaries. I had asked reception about going to Belfast Castle and was told that it was 10 pounds by tax. That morning I asked reception to call me a taxi, and I was off to Belfast Castle. Getting to Belfast Castle is a short journey. From the freeway or motorway, the taxi driver pointed out the majestic looking castle on the hill. Once there, it has splendid views of the Irish Sea, it really gave me that feeling one gets with a romantic kiss. However, the castle is mostly used for functions, weddings, and, being such a romantic place, understandably so. I went inside and there was one attendant in the castle. There was a direct phone to call a cab. It was Value Cab that picked me up but there name is slightly misleading. The car that picked me up was a BMW, and the driver was very serious. I did ask him a few questions as he did not take the highway back, like what areas we were passing through. We finally did strike up a conversation, and I said Belfast is really not that big. He said, "It is not—it's a bit of the same size as Liverpool." He dropped me near The Hercules. I wandered around the city and found a nice pub on upper Church Street called Bittles Bar. It was finally sunny that day. I ordered a Bushmills single malt and a half pint of IPS. There was a very aged-looking man also sitting outside, smoking a pipe. I said hello, and after about 20 minutes he got up and I said, "You're alright." He looked at what I was drinking. This was around lunchtime, and I was drinking a shot of whiskey on ice and a beer. He looked at my drinks and said, "You're alright, you're laughing." The drink made me a bit sleepy, and I went back to my hotel. After a few hours rest, I wanted to venture out for my dinner. Last night I ate at my hotel. I remembered seeing a chain type restaurant called Granny Annie's Kitchen. I gave it a try, and it was very good. I ordered a steak and kidney pie and half a pint of IPA on tap. It was 18 pounds, which is around what I have been paying for a meal in Belfast. I left a 20 pound note, and the waitress told me, "Thanks a million." Many of the people who served me in Belfast were very grateful for my patronage and that I came to Belfast.

Day 17: July 12, Diaries. After staying at the more modest Ramada Inn for four nights, I booked two nights at the Malmaison Hotel. It was just a few hundred feet from my hotel, but I was not aware of this until I passed it on the way back to the Ramada last night. Since I checked in left luggage at Paddington, I had only my hard-to-miss Union Jack with newspaper covered suitcase and my backpack with a plastic carrier bag filled with leaflets about information of museums and historic places to visit, Americans call these pamphlets. When I walked into the hotel, there were two staff to check me in, one serious and one friendly. I went with the friendly one and asked if it was possible to get a cab to Carrickfergus Castle, which is about eight or nine miles outside of Belfast. She gave it her best shot, but there were marches all over Belfast that day. It is almost like Independence Day in the United States. Most roads are blocked off. I wanted to go in the afternoon, after getting some rest, but no chance; it had to be in an hour or so, and I was just way too tired. With blonde hair and her blue glittering eyes, she looked disappointed for me. I said, "It's alright, really." She asked what newspaper I wanted in the morning, and I asked for an *Irish Times*. When I got up to the room, it gave me a feeling of comfort and calm, as the bed had a frame that was a couple of feet high and the room had a mini bar and a wide selection of teas, even tea from Yorkshire. It was the last room in the hall with a window. I could see the top of the brick tower clock.

I had just settled in when I heard the marches in the distance. I rested for a while and then had a walk around town. Most of the streets were deserted until I got to the high street, and there were the marches. The marchers were all men, most with orange banners around them. It was almost like a division or group of men, displaying a big banners. The one that struck me the most was "for God and Ulster." I thought this is very serious patriotism. The United States came to mind, but in the rest of the UK, it's a bit more subtle than this. I think "God Save the Queen" is only played at commemorative events, such as of Her Majesty's reign. Most pubs were closed, and this was a bit disappointing. I resorted to having lunch at a Friday's restaurant in Victoria Shopping Center. I ordered a kamikaze and a French dip, which both were pretty good, but then I ordered one of these fancy drinks called the Purple Rain: Bacardi rum vodka, peach schnapps, blue curacao, sweet and sour mix, 7-Up, and grenadine. I had two sips and could not even drink the rest. It was the only disappointing drink I have had on the tour. Better to stick with Bushmills. Anyway, it was a laid back day. It was around 3 p.m., so I thought I would rest for the day. Finally, for my last day I wanted to make my way up the Causeway.

Day 18: July 13, Diaries: It was my last full day in Belfast. I had rested yesterday, so I was up and ready to go at 5:30 a.m. I got dressed and off I went to the Belfast Central Train Station. I had bought a rail link ticket for Tuesday, as I thought I was going that day, but I never used it. For just 13 pounds one can travel on any bus or train to just about anywhere. I was at the station so early that the ticket counter was not open yet. I went to the gate and I told the attendant that I had not used the card. He checked it and said it was not updated and I had to go to the ticket counter. It had just turned 6:00 a.m., so now the ticket counter was open. The attendant updated the ticket for free. I took the first train out at 7:20 and had to get off at Coleraine, which was the seventh stop. It took an hour and ten minutes to get there and from Coleraine I took a taxi to Dunluce Castle, which is where I wanted to go. As I had set off so early, the castle had not opened yet, but I could have a look at some of it.

The castle is in ruins, but is on the cliffs and has breathtaking views. Although a calm day, I could still hear the waves crashing into the rocks as I look forty or fifty feet down. It was still only 9:20 a.m. by the time I looked around, so I waited until 10: 00 a.m. for the castle to open. A Mercedes taxi pulled up and an Asian family got out of the car. I gave "an alright" to the driver, and then the family went on to look at the castle. I had a chat with him, and he said he was giving them a tour from Belfast for 200 pounds!! When the castle opened, I had a brief look round, but I had already taken a lot of pics, so it did not take me long to finish.

By 10:15, I was ready to move on, but I was in the middle of nowhere with no working phone. The cabbie who drove me said the nearest town was called Portrush. So, I started to walk. After about 15 or 20 minutes, the views of the cliffs were amazing. After about a half an hour of walking, a male walker came up to me. I asked him, "How far is the next town?" He said, "You're a bit far off, about three miles." I said, "What else can I do?" He replied, "Just keep going, Man!" Here I was in the middle of nowhere. I could have accidently gone missing, or if I wanted to purposely go missing, with my mother who is seventy, a brother in Michigan, and my extended family in Yorkshire, who would come find me here?? But I did what the boy told me, I just kept going, Man! I turned around after about forty minutes I saw the castle in the distance, beautiful, just a spectacular view. After an hour, I saw a sign that said "Portrush one mile." My knees started to hurt. I thought one was going to give out. I am a 48-year-old guy with a physical injury. Buses and cars kept zooming past, and when they did, I would hold onto the railing. I did see a hotel on a hill, but I just kept going. I made it to Portrush after an hour and a half's walk.

I saw a hotel. There was a woman outside, next to a bar, sweeping. I asked her if I could get a drink. She said she was not sure as the hotel was not open until noon. I went into the hotel and asked the receptionist. She was not that helpful and a bit curt. "Yes, the kitchen does not serve food until 12:00," she said. I asked, "How far is the next place for food?" She said, "About five minutes." I walked for five minutes and saw no place to eat. By then I had started to feel physically ill. I turned around and went back to the hotel. I used the restaurant toilet and the color of my urine was very yellow. I was dehydrated. I went back, and the first lady, dressed in an open sweat shirt and a tank top, said she would get me a drink of water. She did. I drank it, felt better, and kept on going to the center of the city. I asked an old-age pensioner where I could get something to eat, and indirectly got the same response I had received from the passerby: "Keep going." I made it to the town and found a restaurant called Spinnaker. I had scampi and coleslaw. And just as every time on this trip, for dessert, I ordered sticky toffee pudding. I took a cab back to Colerain Station. As I waited for my train, I had a brief chat with two old-age pensioners. One of them told me that he worked for His Majesty for 35 years. I asked what he did. He replied, "Very little." The train trip there and back to Belfast was 112 miles. I had now traveled 2,340 miles. It was one of the finest, if not the best, days of this trip.

Day 18: July 13, Refection's. I took a rather long gaze at Dunluce Castle as it was behind me. Then, just before I started to walk, I could hear those crashing waves against the rocks, and I took a look at that shiny green grass. The breeze that blew was fresh, as if it was the start of a new day or a new beginning. I had another look back again. I did not see a soul. In the far distance one can see Scotland. There is a reason that the mythic idea of leprechauns came from a country like Ireland. It could be the history of the country, the culture of storytelling, the political struggle, the demise and then the revision of the Gaelic language, or the countryside that is open and desolate. When one looks at open barren land, the mind can drift and not make rhyme from reason. Some of these may be attributes that contributed to the myth of the Irish. Many great Irish writers wrote about it. A romantic idea interpreted from lowbrow of green goblins and ghouls to a serious one that had people dying for their country. The latter is political, but the former I can understand. It is this romantic myth of Ireland that has been a source of inspiration for the Irish both at home and abroad. At that time, not sure if it was myth, or the idea of getting lost, or the emotional exhaustion of my impermanent lifestyle that had gotten the best of me. Since I had come to Doha twenty-five friends have come and gone. I have gone through something similar in every country I have lived in. Lots of hellos and goodbyes. Professional and personal. It feels like an emotional revolving door: some friends kept in touch, some friends never kept in touch, some friends have been out of touch, and some friends' whereabouts remain a mystery. I feel like emotional time has been wasted. My childhood friends in the USA are a rock, but it's a place that has a distance of 10,000 miles from Doha, and many years I have spent away from. Not to mention ten close friends and family have died since I came to Doha, too. It has given me a pain, and I just can't get over. However, when I started walking from Dunluce Castle to Portrush, my neoromantic thought process about myth and Ireland became a hard reality. When I asked the boy that I passed how far the nearest town is and he told me about three miles off, I was not too concerned. However, after 45 minutes or so, when my knees started to hurt, I thought— and I say this in layman's language—if one of my knees blow out, I could be physically injured. I just might really get stuck up here or would have to wave a car down and might end up in an ambulance. This happened to me in Doha when I was carrying my son Kasey. I ended up in an ambulance and paralyzed for 30 minutes. I thought of my wife, Melissa, and that if something happened to me, I would not be able to say goodbye. I think maybe my father would be the only brave soul to rescue me. I think to this day that he was the best friend I ever had. I miss my father.

Day 19: July 14, Diaries. My last day in Belfast. I checked one of my social media sites, and I had an unread a message from my friend Robert, who I was supposed to stay with. Too bad I am leaving. The security at Belfast airport was US-style, I had to go through a machine and put my arms up. And then afterwards, I got patted down. I asked the security guard, "Did you fix my collar?" He replied, "I just did, My Brother." The people of Belfast are so nice, kind, and will talk to anybody. The 458-mile trip from Belfast put me now at 2,798 UK miles traveled.

I landed at Heathrow. With flights inside the UK, passports are not checked. My bag came down the belt ten minutes later. Away I was, at least so I thought. During the summer season, London hotels are overpriced. A four-star hotel can easily cost 200 pounds. I still had a week left on my journey, so I booked an airport hotel for a few nights. It was 100 pounds per night. I tried to take the airport bus to the hotel, but it stopped, or at least this particular one did, after a certain time. I went get a taxi, but the cabbie wanted the address, and I did not have it. I asked him how much it would cost, but he would not tell me. What I needed was a born-and-bred Londoner, because I could tell this guy wasn't. I went back to look for the bus and then had another go with the cabs. I told the guy managing the cabs that the driver did not know the address. He told me to get in the second cab in line, so I pulled my trolley up and got in the cab. While the cabbie put my luggage in, I heard a "Fuckin' Hell!" I got my born and bred Londoner! But I kept quiet and put my guard up while he drove. Before we reached the hotel, which was only a mile away from Heathrow, the Holiday Inn Eriel, he said, "It's just up here, Sir, and there is a very good pub up the road called The Pheasant." I let him know what I was thinking. I said, "You're a born-and-bred Londoner, I can tell." I thanked him, tipped him, and knew I was home.

Day 19: Reflections. The people of Belfast use words like "Man" and "Brother." The later one used by airport security!! I have been to the Republic of Ireland four times, and obviously now to the North, who were exceptionally friendly people. However, the people of Belfast suffered greatly, in the time called The Troubles, which started in 1969. For the next twenty years, robberies, bombs, British troops and checkpoints, rubber bullets used by British soldiers, and petrol bombs by those resisting, were a part of common daily life. Belfast was a major industrial city as early back as the 1870s and this led to many Catholics who lived in rural areas to migrate for work in Belfast. However, during the time of The Troubles, for both Catholics and Protestants unemployment was very high, and to my knowledge the city did not have a thriving tourist's trade. Despite all this, it passed, and the people of Belfast "just kept going." I felt a warmhearted welcome and goodbye from almost everyone I met there. It's the people of Belfast and one unnamed stranger that inspired me to write this book. So I have dedicated it to them.

Day 20: July 15, Diaries. I was exhausted now from my travels. This is now twenty days, and including miles from Doha, almost six thousand miles I have traveled. I fell asleep at 9:00 p.m., woke up at 8:00 a.m., caved in and ate a hotel breakfast, went back to bed, and then woke up at 10:00 a.m. I did not have the stamina to go into London, but knew I would go bonkers if I stayed in my airport hotel all day. So as sad it sounds, I thought I would go to the airport and get something to eat. There were tourists waiting for one of these hop-on, hop-off buses. I waited for a few minutes for one. It pulled up and I asked the driver if he was going to Terminal 2. He said, "This is not the bus you want; I go to Terminal 5." I said, "Oh yes, it takes about 30 minutes to get there." And it does. Heathrow Airport is not your standard, one-building airport. There are several dozen airport hotels, five terminals, and millions of travelers come through every year. The driver said to take a bus across the street. I did, and used an

Oyster card, which a card that can be used on all buses and London underground that can be topped up from five pounds to fifty. The bus ride to Heathrow cost less than two pounds. I hopped off the bus to an airport hotel, which was five pounds, and took a taxi for 15 to 25 pounds. I bought a few items for lunch and went back to the hotel. After a few hours rest, I thought I might go search for the pub that the London cabbie had recommended. I asked about it at my hotel. They actually had a map for it. It is Bath Road and on West End Lane. Very good pub. I only had now my usual scotch and a beer, but the meals for London prices were reasonable and the portion size huge.

Day 21: July 16, Diaries. Felt rested. Went into London at about 10:00 a.m. I did splurge for the Heathrow Express return at 34 pounds. One can travel by underground into Heathrow, but patience is required. It takes about 45 minutes. I had to take pick up some left luggage, so as usual I moved fast. I left it at Paddington, so it was convenient to pick it up, but before I did, I went to my hotel to ask if I could leave my luggage overnight. The receptionist was very nice and said I could. So I went back to Paddington Station, picked up my left luggage, and then dropped it off at my hotel. Now tired!!! One of my favorite local pubs was down the street, the Mitre. I needed a drink and something to eat. They have a sign that says "best Bloody Mary in London." I gave it a try, and not that I have had many in my time, but was it good!!!! I had that and half a roasted chicken. All very good. Total bill was 24 pounds. There and back to Heathrow was 40 miles. This now puts me at 2,838 UK miles traveled.

Day 22 July 17, Diaries. I avoided the breakfast at my hotel and had a walk up the road. I was going to settle for going to McDonalds, but the Sheraton next to my hotel has a Starbucks. I saw a familiarity from my adopted home of Qatar: a crew member of Qatar Airways. I struck up a conversation because I was emotionally and mentally exhausted. I will check into my eighth hotel on this trip today. Checked out of the Holiday Inn Ariel at 11:00 a.m. made it Paddington at about 12:30 p.m. My hotel, the Craven Hotel, is very modest. My room could fit into one of my large bathrooms at my apartment in Qatar. But the sun is shining in London, and it is great weather here. It's the first time I have put a T-shirt on. The Heathrow Express train ride of 20 miles puts me at 2,858 train miles traveled. After sorting out my luggage, I had lunch at a local cafe down the street called Shelia's. Very tiny, but good. For a cup of tea and a sandwich, it was 6 pounds 90 pence.

I wanted to go to the infamous Jermyn Street that is in Piccadilly Circus. It is famous for men's clothing stores. I have been there before, but it's been awhile. When I got to Piccadilly Circus, I ask a few people for the store's location, but no one knew of it. I looked for a well-dressed gentleman. He looked it up and found one on this mobile phone, actually. I asked him where Jermyn Street is, but pronounced it like the male name, and it is not actually. A man overheard us talking and pointed me in the right direction. The first two stores are the slightly cheaper ones, such as Charles Tyrwhitt, and they go up in price as one goes north up the street. I did buy a jacket for 70 pounds, which is not too bad, but I swear it was tagged at 59. To a lifelong Londoner, the heart of the West End is not the place to go. Prices can be ridiculous, and one can get ripped off. After I bought the jacket, I needed a cup of coffee, but rushed back to Paddington, to a more modest part of London.

Day 23: July 18, Diaries. Eltham Palace (Royal Palace 1000 to 1600). Lodgings of King Edward. Henry VIII spent his childhood here. In in a lifetime of coming to London, I had never heard of Eltham Palace. There was a pamphlet about it at my hotel, so asked the hotel clerk about it. He was not sure, but the postal code was S9, so we both guessed it was South East London. He looked it up, and there was no Tube (subway) line to get there, so we both thought best to ask at Paddington Train Station. I asked at the ticket counter, and they had no idea. The attendant told me to go to the information desk. I did, but the attendant there did not know, either. He told me to go to tourist information. A very relaxed, very soft-spoken, big-framed guy knew where Eltham Palace is. He said it is very nice there. He told me I had to go to London Bridge and then take a train to Nottingham. So I did that. I remembered that London Bridge is on the Northern Line, but asked an underground attendant, who said, "Go to Baker Street and take the Jubilee Line." I did that, but my mind wandered, so I missed my Tube stop and ended up getting off at Charring Cross. I went back to Baker Street and got the Jubilee Line to London Bridge. When I got off the Tube, I had a quick search for the train. I asked someone where it was, and they pointed me in the right direction. The escalator up to the station takes one to the infamous Shard building.

Since I was a student living in London in the 90s, the station sure had changed. Back then, the station was two attendants behind a glass counter. Now there is a WHSmith, places to eat, and even a men's clothing store, T.M.Lewin. I bought my ticket for Nottingham and had a look at the T.M.Lewin shop. I found the store clerk, working on his own, much friendlier than those on Jermyn Street. He had some nice shirts on sale. The shirts I looked at a few of the shops on Jermyn were plain and common, really. I could get them anywhere. I wanted one with the stiff collar and stripes. I have been dressing more casual than I used to, growing up in my overtly preppy home town of Grosse Pointe Farms, Michigan. I wanted to return to my roots. There was one to my liking, and the store clerk was very friendly. I told him what happened in the shop yesterday. He said if an item is tagged that should be the price. I mentioned that people can get ripped off in the West End. They probably thought I was some tourist, unfamiliar with London.

After I bought my shirt, I got on the train to Nottingham. I asked an attendant which platform, which was number 7. When I stood by the train platform, there was a man whose job it is to hold a sign that the train can depart. I mentioned to him how much the train station has changed. He said The Shard tower was built by the Saudis. I politely corrected him and said, "Qataris." He mentioned that it was they who had invested the money to clean up the train station to make it "look more presentable." I thought how interconnected the world is. The train ride to Nottingham took just ten minutes, and after going the wrong way, again I had a conversation with a local. He said, "You are going to have to go up the other hill." I finally made it to the place. The gardens are beautiful. With a moat surrounding the castle and a chapel attached—it's quite spectacular! However, inside there are not that many rooms to see. And the audiovisual guide was actually confusing. It was not the standard "just press the number shown in the room." However, it was worth the trip just to have a look at the majestic gardens.

Day 23: July 19, Diaries. Laid back day, today. Went to Hampstead Heath to visit my friend James. I went book shopping there and I bought two more books: Ivan Turgenev's *Fathers and Sons* and *The Diary of Anne Frank*. My book count is up to seventeen now. James and I spent a nice evening in Hampstead Heath at a pub called the Garden Green.

Day 23: July 19, Reflections. Hampstead is a North London suburb that has an Underground Tube station called West Hampstead. The high street in Hampstead has good pubs, some charity shops, and restaurants. There is an over-ground railway station. Take the train from this station, and in just one stop, one can visit Hampstead Heath. There are quaint pubs scattered around the area, like the one James and I went to. The pub had a big garden, but tucked away with green plush plants hanging overhead. This area was full of patrons drinking and dining, enjoying themselves to the fullest, and during the middle of the week, too. Hampstead has some very expensive flats (hardly any to purchase under 1 million pounds). It has a large, green hill area for walking, called the Hampstead Heath Common. This was a favorite place to visit of the pop icon George Michael, although his reasons for visiting were slightly different than mine, as it was rumored he cruised the common. Regardless, I feel quite honored that we shared a similar London hangout. Although an impermanent and an unsettled life, which has led me to change countries like most people do automobiles, I have led a privileged one.

Day 24 : July 20. My Social Media post today.

Captain's Log Day 24. After visiting 10 cities in three weeks (London three times), when I came into central London on Monday I was mentally and physically exhausted, but the weather was very good and the sun was shining. So far this is the only place in the UK that has been warm. The sun always shines on London, maybe because the Queen lives here. It was the first time so far I have been able to wear T-shirts, so on Monday I wore my Hard Rock Cafe Warsaw shirt and on Tuesday my Keith Richards "I am still alive 2017" T-shirt. The weather perked me up. I saw a leaflet for Elham Palace. Just when I thought I have done everything in London (not sure if I flew into Manchester or Heathrow, but my first trip to the UK by myself was when I was twelve years old), I decided to have a day trip to Eltham Palace….. When I got to Eltham Palace, I found the gardens are beautiful, and so is the exterior of the palace. The inside of the palace is fair, really, with small rooms and 1930s décor, but then again my childhood friends who remember the estate of my late, great father, know that when it comes to estates, let's just say I have high standards. It was my father's birthday on Monday, and I have thought about him a lot on this trip. I am sure he would be astounded by how much I have been traveling recently and ecstatic about my desire to write and publish as much as I can. Thinking of him.

Day 24: Reflections. In 1985 my father bought the Deming Estate on Lakeshore Drive in the prestigious Detroit suburb of Grosse Pointe Farms. The house was nothing short of spectacular. When visitors came to my childhood home, I often heard various phrases to describe the estate: "This house is huge," "Ohh my god," "incredible," and "What a home!" With a modest forty-nine rooms, the black-and-grey Tudor had nine front windows and stood majestically a hundred yards back off Lake St. Clair, with a yard as long as a football field. Now looking back, it's as if driving up the driveway was a visit back in time to the 1920s. There was a circular rose garden in front and ivy on the stone chimney, which stood all three stories on the estate. It was built at the turn of the twentieth century. It had a majestic ballroom, eight bedrooms on the front side of the home, and half a dozen in the rear wing of the home. My brother Nick and I had the third floor to ourselves, which had separate bedrooms, a bathroom, a lounge room that was painted pink, and a large, long room with wood floors that my brother sand blasted and varnished one summer. The basement had an old fashioned boiler and walk-in safe. My father, an avid gardener, put a pond in the backyard with a rock waterfall, water lilies, and Japanese koi fish. There were also several grape vines in the backyard. Although no wine was ever made, my father and my stepmother did make fresh grape juice from the grapes one summer. My father even put up chicken wire in a room adjacent to the kitchen and filled it with canary birds. He also bought a peacock, which lived in a fenced area next to the pond. With lineage of my father's father being Indian Rajput, he took himself back to his aristocratic roots, although Dad kept himself humble and his expenses down by doing a majority of the work on the estate himself. I contributed, as my brother and I would cut the grass on a big John Deere tractor. The financial maintenance of the home was $10,000 per month ($21,000 in today's money). Unfortunately, my father sold the estate in 1998 due to gradually escalating high property taxes. The estate was demolished by a developer who built several modern homes on the land.

Day 25: July 21, Diaries. This was the social media post today. Goodbye to the United Kingdom! I have done trips of this length with my father to Pakistan and a few times with my wife to the United States, but this one included eight hotels, 3,000 UK miles, and ten cities. It's over and it's been great. There is good and bad just about everywhere, but I met a wide variety of people of different races, religions, and social classes, and they were all welcoming. This next story never happened to me before. The taxi driver who took me to the airport was from Afghanistan, and when I told him about my father, he did not want to take the cab fare!

However, the city I will never forget is Belfast, and when I was up the Causeway in the middle of nowhere, stuck with no phone or ride, and got an emotional uplift from a perfect stranger. "Just keep on going, Man!" That really is metaphor for the people of Belfast. Despite suffering internal conflict for many years, they just kept going, and most were very nice people. While hardly the same type of suffering, I can understand. I have spent 20 years living in seven different countries away from the United States and my immediate family. Despite traveling as many air miles as a senior airline pilot, just like most of us, I have had my share of ups and downs, but I just kept going. I was going to wait for my autobiography to tell it all, but will go ahead and publish my diaries of this trip, which include travel tips, stories of my experience of visiting every country in the UK (except for Wales), my story of an emotional search, and reuniting with old friends, a sort of homecoming. In the meantime, thanks for listening and following me while I was on the road, and let's all just keep going, Man!

When I had checked into my flight at Heathrow, I mentioned that I had already checked in on line, but that I wanted to change my seat. (As I am a creature of routine, and have flown Qatar Airways over one hundred times, they expect me and usually put me in row 15.) I asked if there was anything closer to the front, and the flight attendant said a few seats that were blocked off in the 30s rows, but her supervisor had to give approval, and he was not available at the moment. When I got to the gate and asked again, the attendant said the row 30s seats are in the upper deck and not available. The attendant apologized to me. And I replied, "It's alright." As a Qatar Privilege Club member, I went into the priority boarding line. As the attendant scanned my passport, he said, "Come with me." I thought maybe I was in trouble, because when going through security, an officer told me that placing items on a tray is "not rocket science," so I told him how rude he was. Then the attendant said, "You have been upgraded." He put me in the business class line!!! There were two attendants waiting there, and they said, "We are not boarding yet." I was so excited, I just started rambling on and on about how many flights I have taken and it's never happened before. They both just stood there and smiled at me.

When I boarded the plane, they escorted me to the very front seat, and the flight attendant said, "Take a seat, Mr. Jan." I just could not believe it; I got a bit teary eyed with joy. I was offered many different newspapers and picked up a *Telegraph* and had a read. Then I wrote some of this last log in my diary. When the plane took off, I started to read one of the books I bought in Hampstead, *Fathers and Sons* by Ivan Turgenev. That worked for a while, but as soon as the seatbelt sign went off, I was given a menu and ordered a glass of champagne, then another one. Then here comes the chief steward. "Mr. Jan another glass of champagne?" he asked. "It's on us!!" By this time *Fathers and Sons* became blurry, and I put it down. I was asked when I would like to eat. I said in a few hours. I ordered salmon on diced potato salad for starter, lamb for main course, and lemon tart for dessert. It was all fantastic. I had four flight attendants wait on me, and they all made sure I kept hydrated with water and cups of tea. I just jammed out to the variety of rock artists: Bruce Springsteen, The Clash, and Oasis. I reclined my seat all the way back and put my feet up the rest of the way home.

At the end of the flight, as now at the end of all my Qatar Airways flights, the chief steward came to my seat asked me how the flight was. I said, "Spectacular." He asked me if I would fill out a comment card, and I showed some good manners by saying I will give the names of all the staff that waited on me. It was a great way to end an amazing trip. It is not uncommon for most of the professional classes and working classes too, taking up to a month's holiday. So that was one purpose, and the other to reunite with old friends. It was also a sort of a homecoming too, but this was my tenth trip to the UK in the last six years, I really have been on one perpetual homecoming. No noncitizen of any Gulf country gets lifelong residency or the passport, so I was also searching. At least on an emotional basis I was lost, but now I have been found.

Back in Doha: It is always good to come back to Doha, there is an e-gate system for residents and Qatari citizens. After passengers have cleared immigration and have a security check of the bag they are carrying, there is always several staff to answer questions, if one needs help. However, now most all my friends have left Doha. Many I met through my wife, as they were her colleagues at Qatar Foundation. Some I worked with at one of the American universities here, Texas A&M at Qatar, and some I worked with at Berlitz Language School. Others I played squash with. Most are gone. To say it is isolating would be an understatement. In the compound where I live, no one walks, and one can only see cats outside. Virtually no people. The first week back, I had two phone conversations with a friend. In this world of instant messaging, itself an impersonal and isolating way of communicating, I initiated the phone conversation just to speak to a human being. Worse, as a traveler I took some sleeping pills with me, but I was so active on my trip that I hardly used them, but back in Doha, I took some to sleep and it was a nightmare to come off them. Many nights I lay awake until 3:00 a.m. I did work with my assistant and then have dinner with a friend, so daily life improved a bit after a week. My family came home from their trip to the US, and I was glad to see them, but life still remained isolating. I still could not sleep. I would lay in bed and then wake up at about 12 noon or 1:00 p.m. and eat. I stopped taking sleeping pills, but this pattern continued for a couple more days. Then one afternoon, when Melissa and I took Kasey to McDonald's, as I stood in line, I heard a dozen or so voices in my head, and tension all over my body. I thought I was having a heart attack. I drank the water I ordered with my meal, then needed another bottle, then another. My wife looked at my face and calmly said I would be okay. I started to feel better, and got another bottle of water. After all this water, I went to the bathroom, and I was severely dehydrated. That was it. (Temperatures were 40-plus Celsius/110 Fahrenheit.) I still did not sleep well for days. Also on my trip I had taken a few Xanax, too. Then, on top of that, my wife and I were adjusting to being home together with nobody else around.

The drugs I mentioned are very serious, and one must consult a medical professional before taking or getting off these pills. As for hydration, lots of water or tea. I finally settled down after about three weeks. One month later, the boy up the Causeway's words still remain with me: "Just keep going, Man." Words that have been a source of inspiration for me and in my thoughts often, from times that I have been on the treadmill and thought about stopping and even for writing this book. Adversity is a part of life, but it should not stop any of us from reaching for our hopes and dreams. Despite adversity, I am happy to say many of my dreams have been reached and lived. That's expat life—it is fast, adventurous, interesting, lonely, tiring, thrilling, heartbreaking, and challenging. And that's my story about a two-month summer experience from June and July of 2017.

Figure one. My first trip to Edinburgh with my brother Nick and my father in 1986.

Figure 2The View of the special mountain from my hotel in Corstorphine.

Figure 3 Town of Corstorphine, UK

Figure 4 Church in Christropihine

Figure 5 Dinner with Karen and James at a French restaurant, the name of the restaurant was a big surprise!

Figure 6 Me at the Isle of Sky. This was supposed to be on my cover but I went with the generic cover. I am an independent author and putting my first book together I was kind of, so to speak, going through the midst.

Figure 7 Sticky Toffee Pudding - a UK dessert.

Figure 8 Edinburgh Castle

Figure 9 Duke of Wellington statue at Glasgow Art museum.

Figure 10 Inverness. The church in the background that walked to.

Figure 11 Isle of Sky

Figure 12 Isle of Skye

gure 13 Helen and I in Newcastle.

Figure 14 Picture next page. Dinner with Helen and Richard at Portofino's Italian restaurant.

Figure 15 Rachel took this picture after our Lunch at a resturant called the Happy Place.
How appropraite.

Figure 16 St. Nicholas Catherdral Newcastle.

Figure 17

Figure 18 Murial in East Belfast

Figure 19 Murial in West Belfast

Figure 20 Dulance Castle where I got lost

Figure 21 Belfast Castle

Figure 22 My childhood home in Grosse Pointe Michigan, USA.

Figure 23 I liked Scotland as it reminded me of this trip to Gilgit, Pakistan with my family when I was 19.

.

Figure 22 Great way to End my trip with an upgrade to business class.

Made in the USA
Middletown, DE
20 May 2018